Flip ~~~

Prepare yourself for a magnificent journey. Go into the unknown with Karen and experience unexpected discoveries . . . fast, easy, and fun!

Allow Karen to guide you on your Heroine's Journey. Her insight, wisdom, and courage will demonstrate, "If she can do it, you can do it too!"

I have watched Karen apply everything she teaches in this book. Her results are miraculous, magical, and magnificent! If she can do it, you can do it too!

> Moira Lethbridge, M.Ed.
> Author-Speaker-Facilitator-Executive Coach, Lethbridge & Associates LLC

Flip Time / Love Life is an engaging, powerful, and inspirational parable full of incredible wisdom and ways to be authentically happy in the present, all the while reaching for more meaning and expansive personal challenges. Karen shares so much knowledge, empowerment, and applicable tools, strategies, and tips to uncover the happiness we all desire. This story reveals the real secret we are longing for: how to become connected to your best self and higher purpose. *Flip Time / Love Life* is a beautiful and uplifting short story for all ages and generations.

> Julie Reisler
> Life Designer™
> Author, TEDx Speaker, Podcast Host, Lululemon Ambassador

I have had the privilege of a front-row seat, watching Karen Briscoe lead a life of intention, transformation, and expansion. Finally, she's made it available to all of us, with this beautifully written story. Inside are the keys to actively shaping your personal evolution, elevating what is possible, and living the life you were meant to lead.

Jon Berghoff
The Collective Intelligence Whisperer
Co-founder and managing partner, the Flourishing Leadership Institute

Flip Time is a seemingly simple concept that has profound implications for your life, work, and relationships. The characters and situations in author Karen Briscoe's parable will be reminiscent to many of us who've woken up in midlife, wondering how we got so busy yet not seeming to get the important things done. As the saying goes, everyone is necessarily the hero of their own life story. This book will leave you inspired to set big goals and dreams, knowing that you can achieve them with the strategies the main character, Haley, discovers and uses for herself along her—and your—Heroine's Journey. It's about time.

Carol Cox
Founder, Speaking Your Brand

As I turned the pages of *Flip Time / Love Life*, I felt as though Karen Briscoe had put my life, fears, and challenges directly on the pages. This book captures the struggles and victories of the Heroine's Journey as she discovers that committing to positive action is the key to future happiness and success. This book takes the reader through the discovery that you can break through any obstacles and you can have the life of your dreams by simply FLIPPING TIME AND LOVING LIFE!

> Christy C. Solar
> Fairway Independent Mortgage Corporation
> Team Solar, Senior Loan Officer

Talk about perfect timing! Karen Briscoe has created a story so real, depicting what many of us have gone through in our entrepreneurial and classic life adventures. Regardless of where you are in life's journey, this book is a good fit for you. If you are a lifelong student of learning, *Flip Time / Love Life* is for you. Hold on tight as Karen and her divinely tuned characters take you through life's challenges. Plenty of lessons to be learned; be prepared to take a lot of notes. This is a must read!

> Doug Sandler
> Founder, TurnKey Podcast Productions, and author, *Nice Guys Finish First*

Before I even finished **Flip Time / Love Life**, I knew it was the kind of book I will return to again and again to soak up all its meaningful nuggets of wisdom. No matter where you are on your own journey, Briscoe's compelling words will transport you into the Heroine's Journey, inspiring you to know you are capable of breaking through any obstacle holding you back from getting to "be your highest and best self, the person you are meant to be."

Linda McKissack
National bestselling author of *Hold*
Creator and co-host of *Everything Life and Real Estate* podcast

You make choices from the moment you wake each morning. Are your choices supporting your bliss? Karen's book is about doing just that. This story takes you on a call to adventure. To love the life you have while you create the life of your dreams. To be the kind of person who does meaningful work and activities to have bliss.

Moneeka Sawyer
Blissfulinvestor.com
Bestselling author of *Choose Bliss: The Power and Practice of Joy and Contentment*
Host of *Real Estate Investing for Women* on iTunes

Where do I begin! So many important life lessons, reflections, and impactful stories in this book. We all have the same amount of time in each day, but how we "view it" to get the most out of our lives is where the magic is. Karen helps us understand this in her "magical" book, ***Flip Time / Love Life.*** This book truly will stand the test of time. With each reread, the reader gleams new insights to get the most out of life! Thank you for writing this book, Karen!

Jennifer Abernethy
Socially Delivered

With courage and joyous effort, Haley models how one resilient woman can move from success to significance, making the world a better place while enjoying the ride. Inspiring and useful, ***Flip Time*** rings a lot of bells. The story is filled with wisdom, zest and practical tools for addressing the habits and behaviors most likely to undermine successful women. I loved, felt inspired by, and learned from Haley's remarkable journey.

Sally Helgesen,
Author of *How Women Rise* and *The Female Advantage*

Flip Time! Love Life

A Heroine's Journey

A 5 MINUTE SUCCESS STORY

KAREN BRISCOE

5
MINUTE PRESS

Start today!

Dedication

This book is dedicated to:

My dad and mom, who were my first cheerleaders
and role models of what success looks like.

My husband, Andy, who has encouraged me to
achieve success in all areas of my life and work.

Our children, Drew and Callie, who have brought both
joy and challenge to my life
beyond what I ever dreamed possible.

And to you, the reader:

Here's to your Heroine's Journey!
FLIP TIME / LOVE LIFE

*Here's to your
Call to Adventure!*

Karen Buscia

Table of Contents

Flip Time / Love Life

FOREWORD, BY HAL ELROD

As cliché as it may sound, every single one of us deserves to love the life we have *while* we create the life of our dreams, and yet very few come close. Most people seem to settle for less than what we really want (and deserve), never tapping into our inborn ability to design our lives to be what we want them to be. Every single one of us is just as worthy, deserving, and capable of creating anything we choose as any other person on earth. It's up to us.

Through dedicating the majority of my adult life to studying human potential and optimizing it through personal development, I am sold on the belief that regardless of where we are in our lives, we have the potential to take all areas of our lives to new levels of success and fulfillment.

It seems that most people never take the time to really identify exactly what they want their lives to look like. They have general ideas . . . I want more time . . . I want more money . . . I want to be happier . . . I know I should be healthier. However, despite these vague ambitions, most of us just take whatever comes our way and accept it as our reality. Oftentimes we fill our hours and days with things that we don't really care about and don't really matter, crowding out and taking up space from things that do. Sometimes we even attach a negative meaning from it, which can make our lives seem insignificant or troubled. We all go through things that may not be ideal, but we all have the ability to decide how we react to them and assign our life experiences any meaning we choose.

Do you LOVE the life you have? If not, do you want to? Do you constantly say you are too busy and don't have time to do something meaningful? If so, reading this book is your first step.

Karen shared the *Flip Time / Love Life* message to a crowd of 450 people at the Best Year Ever Blueprint live event in San Diego in December 2018 and received a standing ovation. She has also been a committed member of the Quantum Leap Mastermind (QLM) community for several years.

In this book, Karen shares *Flip Time / Love Life,* a Heroine's Journey story. The message is a tale that allows you, as the reader, to immerse yourself in the experience. Countless personal development, self-help, and similar genres offer information. Illustrating through story has been proven to bypass our analytical/critical mind and reside more deeply in our subconscious, thus making a deeper and lasting impact. The impact is at an emotional level rather than "how-to" instructions. This is why legends, parables, myths, and allegories have stood the test of time. New insights and applications are gleaned as one goes back and reads and rereads. The book uses the *Wizard of Oz* characters and story as an analogy.

It's up to you to make a decision to take action, design a life you love, and start living it today! Reading this book is your first step.

With Love and Gratitude,
Hal Elrod
#1 bestselling author, *The Miracle Morning*

A Note to the Reader
FROM THE AUTHOR, KAREN BRISCOE

Before we begin, it may be helpful for you, as the reader, to have some background on how this book came about. I wrote my first book, ***Real Estate Success in 5 Minutes a Day,*** to help people, particularly real estate agents, achieve a higher level of success in their business and lives. The idea was to bust the myth that people didn't have enough time to invest in their business and personal development. All it took was JUST five minutes a day to have a positive effect.

My goal at that time was to impact the more than *two million real estate agents* licensed in the United States as well as related industry professionals. To do that, I spoke to countless groups of agents, lenders, title company representatives, home inspectors, stagers, and others closely connected to the industry. I have been interviewed on hundreds of podcasts and participated in countless webinars.

What I found is that the principles of **5 Minute Success** applies across the board to sales professionals, entrepreneurs, and to just about any business endeavor. The crazy thing is that it also applies to authors, speakers, coaches, and even nonprofits.

This made me realize that my potential reach was way beyond real estate and ancillary industries and professions. That is when the **5 Minute Success** podcast was born. The guests on the podcast include top-ranking real estate professionals, lenders, authors, podcast hosts, speakers, nonprofit founders, and leaders in countless industries. The breadth and depth continues to expand. The podcast has ranked as the #1 most recommended business podcast on Overcast and is proud to be a part of the Turnkey Production Group, which boasts over two million downloads.

The book as a daily reader consistently ranks in the top 1 percent on Amazon in its category and was selected in an INMAN article as the top book to read for 2017. What I found is that many people find it challenging to make a daily commitment for an entire year. That led to the creation of the **66 Day Challenge®** books; the first in the series was **Commit to Get Leads**. The **66 Day Challenge®** online courses offer a jump-start in the particular area one wants to focus on.

All this is good, and yet I knew there was something more that was mine to contribute. My personal and company mission is to impact and improve people's lives. That goes beyond being highly productive. That is what led to **Flip Time / Love Life**.

In so many conversations, I heard from people that they too want to be successful in the professional realm AND live a full life. They wanted to know how I do it. How I put meaningful work and activity first. How it has improved my life, as well as those around me.

This mission is about as broad as it can get. Once you **FLIP TIME**, you will **LOVE** the **LIFE** you have as you create and co-create the life of yours dreams. That is truly the top of the pyramid!

A Heroine's Journey

Flip Time / Love Life is the story of a Heroine's Journey. As a tale, it allows you, the reader, to immerse yourself in the experience. Although personal development, self-help, and similar genres offer information, illustrating through story often can impact at a higher level than "how-to" instructions. This is why parables, allegories, myths, and legends have stood the test of time. One can go back and read and reread and glean new insights and applications. The inspiration for this book came from my life and others who have been on my Heroine's Journey with me.

The majority of the characters and names in the story are essentially a figment of my imagination. The main character is Haley, whose name means heroine. Although the heroine makes do with her ordinary life, she feels as if there is something missing. She ventures outside her comfort zone on a Call to Adventure. On the journey from the known to the unknown, she meets with challenges; takes transformational leaps; and asks for and receives help from friends and guides. As she embraces her full life, she lives into her joy of genius and returns with treasures that empower her to embark on the next call.

The people who have been instrumental in my life's journey are identified in the story by their real names:

- **Moira Lethbridge,** author of *Savvy Woman in 5 Minutes a Day: Make Time for a Life that Matters, The Gift of Receiving,* and my personal executive life coach

- **Julie Reisler,** author of the series *Get a PhD in You* and the voice of *Real Estate Success in 5 Minutes a Day* and *Commit to Get Leads: 66 Day Challenge*, as well as *5 Minute Success—The Podcast* intro and outro

- **Hal Elrod,** author of the *Miracle Morning* series

- **Jon Berghoff**, co-founder and managing partner of the Flourishing Leadership Institute

- **Gay Hendricks,** author of countless books, including *The Big Leap* and *The Zone of Genius*

- **Carol Cox**, founder and podcast host, *Speaking Your Brand*

Annotated quotes are by the "real" person attributed in the story.

The book concludes with reflections on a Heroine's Journey using *The Wizard of Oz* characters and story as an analogy. An analogy is a linguistic tool to transfer meaning and inspiration.

Immense gratitude to all who have impacted and improved my life! I am who I am in many ways because of you and your contribution to my becoming my "highest and best self."

Chapter 1
MEMORIES PRESSED BETWEEN THE PAGES OF MY MIND

THE REARVIEW MIRROR

Haley looks back at the last few years and comes to the conclusion that there are two types of people in the world. One group wonders, "Where did the time go?" She remembers when she used to feel overwhelmed with her busy life and is thankful that her life now is full and meaningful. Truly she has become part of the second group of people: those who love the life they have while they create the life of their dreams.

Those who knew the "before" Haley see the change, too, and inquire, "What's different about her? And, how does she do it all?" Sometimes it seems too good to be true and she feels the need to pinch herself! She believes with her mind, heart, and soul that if she can do it, others can, too. It's never too late to start!

PERHAPS YOU ARE A BIT LIKE HALEY

As a young woman, Haley's journey was like that of many others. Where did it all begin? It was her dream to find love, someone to share the joys and struggles of life with. In the salad days of her career in Denver, she was also pursuing a master's degree at night. It was through mutual friends at church that she was introduced to Clint Beck. Pastor Bill married the young couple a few years later in front of oh, such a great cloud of witnesses.

Clint, the love of her life, was everything she had ever dreamed of in a man. Strong, encouraging, and he made her laugh. They had a standing joke between them that went back to their first unofficial date. Haley had boldly asked Clint why he wasn't married yet, given that he was one of the most eligible guys in the church's singles group. Clint said that he hadn't found anyone who could keep up with him and Haley remarked, "Well, I don't know what the big deal is. I could."

THE SITUATION

Fast forward to two kids, Will and Mattie, and Clint's demanding job in public relations for a multinational company. There never seemed to be the time or money for the two of them to get away, much less for Haley to do anything that she truly wanted to do. The constant feeling of not being in control of her life hit Haley hard as she crossed over the threshold into her forties.

A midlife crisis seemed too much of a classic situation and yet that was what it was. She felt unappreciated. After all, she had put her own life and successful career in finance and accounting on hold while Clint advanced professionally. She was, in effect, a single parent much of the time due to his extensive travel schedule. Hope was on the horizon, though, as the kids became more independent, now thirteen and ten.

THE RE-ENTRY

Haley began to explore reentering the workforce in a more meaningful way than the part-time jobs she had held through the years when the kids were young. Her background as a strong administrator was where her knowledge, skills, and abilities were best suited. And yet, she knew that the real money was in sales, where being commission-based created more financial opportunity and recognition. She just didn't see herself as being a pushy salesperson, though.

She remembered her entrepreneurial father quoting Napoleon Hill: "Don't wait. The time will never be right." So she armed herself with that affirmation and dove right back into the workforce.

THE CONNECTION

Haley was ready for a challenge, so she reached out to several successful women in the community who she was acquainted with from her volunteer work. This led to an opportunity in the mortgage industry to join the team of a mega-producer, Audrey Adler.

Over the next couple years, Haley became well known in the company for her professional consultative approach. She proved her value to the team by being a consistent lead generator, not just a lead receiver. With a servant's heart, her mission was to impact and improve people's lives by helping with their housing financial matters. This put her on Audrey's radar and led to Haley soon after becoming a junior partner.

The real estate market was strong from 2002-2006, which meant the lending environment was favorable as well. Some saw signs of a bubble and perhaps weakening on the horizon in 2007 and early 2008. Audrey recognized that it would be better to join forces with Haley than to later have her as a competitor. When Audrey was diagnosed with breast cancer in 2006, she and her husband knew the time was upon them for succession planning.

THE GOLDEN HANDSHAKE

Audrey knew that Haley had choices. As a producer, she had the ability to rise high as a sole practitioner or could easily be lured away by others. It was prophetic in a way, because just months after executing the golden handshake agreement in the summer of 2008, the financial markets crashed and Audrey passed away.

The next few years were a blur for Haley as she struggled to find the bottom line and keep the business profitable. She realized early on that she didn't want to handle the business alone, so rather than waiting to the end of her career and life as Audrey had, she brought on a junior partner in 2009.

Anne Crawford was sharp, attractive, and a Generation Xer. A strong lead generator in her own right, in just a few years Anne was producing at the same level as Haley. The team kept Audrey's name as part of brand continuity and were affectionately known in the market area as The AHA Group. Their mission was to be like an "aha," a breath of fresh air in the competitive industry.

THE AWAKENING

By this time, Will was in college and Mattie was finishing high school. The year Haley turned fifty was pivotal, as it had been almost a decade since the initial onslaught of her midlife crisis. That year, Clint insisted that, with Anne to hold down the fort, they should take a true vacation, rather than a trip tagged onto one of his business trips. Haley loved to be outdoors and to hike, so they embarked on a luxury walking tour and wine tasting of Italy.

This vacation was a game-changer, as Haley saw that life could be more than the hamster wheel of being only as good as her last deal. It gave her a taste of travel. The only challenge was how to make the time.

A BLOG IS BORN

As a member of her firm's top producer club, Haley had opportunities to mastermind with others in the field across the nation. At a social media training in 2009, Haley made the commitment to write a blog on a weekly basis. This led to recognition outside the firm, and soon she was in demand as a speaker and trainer.

In her travels across the United States, she saw that as one progressed up the ranks of the mortgage industry, there were fewer and fewer women represented. Women consistently outnumbered men in the lower levels and administrative functions. In fact, the numbers flipped; by Haley's estimates, only 20 percent of the top echelon ranks were women.

THE PARADIGM

Another paradigm she saw was that as professionals reached the higher levels, many ventured out into other arenas. Some became team leaders, others went into training or onto the management and oversight track. A few started their own boutique firms.

Haley was most interested in those who had created a "side-hustle" in addition to production. One friend from her mastermind group had written a book, another was on the speaking circuit, others coached. Over and over people told Haley that her stories were "sticky" and memorable and that she should write a book! Although Haley found the idea inspiring, she felt that she already didn't have enough time or money to do what she wanted to do. How would she ever find the time to write a book? Yet the seed was planted.

FAKE IT UNTIL YOU MAKE IT

Productivity was always one of Haley's key strengths. Naturally driven and motivated, Haley discovered that focusing on lead generation and business development had a strong return on investment. As a novice in the business, she almost always out-worked everyone else. Truly, she faked it until she made it. But what she wanted to do, in the words of social psychologist, author, and speaker Amy Cuddy, was to: "Fake it until you become it."

She was ready to take her career to the next level, and she knew what she needed to do. Whenever Haley would hit a ceiling in achievement, it was time to hire a coach or join a mastermind group—and sometimes both! Her intuition told her that to go to the next level, she would require new knowledge, skills, and abilities.

The question perplexed her: What was her next?

THE HIERARCHY OF NEEDS

Looking back, she remembered that sense of satisfaction, that there must be something more. Haley recalled Abraham Maslow's Hierarchy of Needs from a college psychology course and recognized her journey up the pyramid.

Her basic physiological and safety needs never seemed satisfied. There was that nagging sense of desire of always wanting more. She reflected on her first job out of college, when she earned $16,000 a year. It had seemed like a lot of money. Now her personal company credit card bill was that much practically every month!

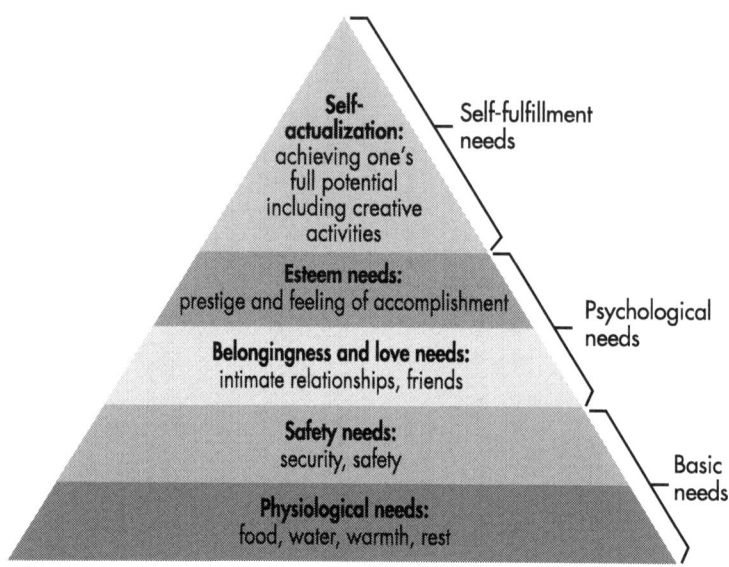

Haley and Clint's marriage was approaching a quarter-century together, and their kids were doing well. So when people asked how she was, it was fairly easy to respond with "Good, but busy." What really had taken off were her esteem needs, which she attributed primarily to her success as a mortgage lender. Truly she felt accomplished in her field and enjoyed an element of prestige as a consistent top producer in the top 1 percent with both her company and the industry.

And yet she had that nagging feeling that there was something more. The hierarchy concept shows how one is supposed to work their way up the pyramid. Only once the lower levels are satisfied could you go on to the next level. The problem was that very few people ever get to the self-actualization step at the top because they run out of time.

To take the next step required traveling to unknown territory. And who really has time for self-actualization?

ENTREPRENEUR BENT

Haley felt from a young age that her natural bent as an entrepreneur came from her father, Lewis Fuller. The Fuller family was well known in the small town of Wimberley, Texas, for the enticing smell of smoked BBQ billowing on the side of the road. Haley's father took the special recipe and brand to the college and capitol town of Austin in a big way. Their trademarked food trucks with the slogan "Fill 'er up on Fuller Famous BBQ" was franchised across Texas and the southwest.

It seemed to Haley that entrepreneurs thrived on a challenge and the excitement of creating and launching a business. Once a concept was in orbit with sustainable, scalable systems, often the entrepreneur became restless. The "next" idea began to ferment and soon the entrepreneur was taking action.

Chapter 2
ONE LIFE FULLY LIVED

THE MEETING

As an active member of the local Chamber of Commerce Board, Haley consistently advocated for empowering local women business owners. The makeup of the board was predominantly men, so along with the president of the Chamber, they reached out to area chambers to create a network known as the Women's Coalition of Influence. At a breakfast meeting, executive life coach Moira Lethbridge shared how she helps women achieve mindful success. Another seed was planted.

Later, over coffee with Moira, Haley shared that she was smack in the middle of busyness and overwhelm, the twins of perfectionism. Something was missing and, as Moira gently probed, Haley revealed her passion to write a book. Many people had told her that she should write one, as she had been writing a blog for a few years, which had achieved recognition on national sites. Haley felt she had a voice and a message.

Moira was curious about what was keeping Haley from realizing her dream. Haley emphasized how very busy she was and that there was never enough time and money. So many people were dependent on her to perform well. Haley said she wanted to write—so why couldn't she just make the time?

UNMET NEEDS AS CLUTTER

At some point, Haley felt she either needed to change her expectations or the timeline. Maybe self-actualization should be put off until after she retired. But she already felt as if she had put her life on hold to raise the kids; waiting might be too late. It actually felt like more work to feel unfulfilled. The frustration of not achieving her heart's desire weighed on her and pulled her down. It was like clutter around the house and office—taking up space but not adding value.

LIFE'S JUNK DRAWER

The situation reminded Haley of one of her favorite movies of all time, **The Intern.** The character played by Anne Hathaway is the founder of a successful online women's clothing company. In the common work room, a table in the main area had become the communal "junk drawer." Every time Hathaway passed it, she promised herself that she would make time to tidy it up.

Fortunately for Hathaway, the intern in the movie saw how it disturbed her and took it upon himself to arrive early and complete the task. Haley didn't think anyone, like the fairy tale "prince charming," was going to come along and do that for her. She was going to need to be her own heroine in her life.

It was just that Haley felt that even procrastination took work and in a way became self-punishing. The voice in her head, her inner critic, was prosecuting her constantly for a litany of deficits. She knew she should be putting her energy toward her wants and positive outcomes rather than wasting time thinking about what might have been.

CHANGE OR DIE

Moira shared from Alan Deutschman's book, **Change or Die**, that when people must make changes due to health reasons, 90 percent cannot accomplish it on their own. Willpower alone is insufficient. For true change to "stick," it requires being in relationship with others who embrace compassionate accountability for each other.

This seemed a little extreme to Haley, who had already accomplished a great deal on her own for some time. She was certain her drive and hard work would overcome inertia and she would figure it out, and thanked Moira for her time.

THE CREATIVE PATTERN

Being in a sales profession, Haley was familiar with the DISC Theory of Behavior by William Marston. She knew without a doubt that her behavioral style was a DC. The D's dominant trait is that of "Dominance," which is a driven, determined, decision-based person who is results-oriented. Her secondary behavioral trait was C, Consciousness, which includes being very precise and detail focused.

The combined behavioral traits can appear schizophrenic. Those who knew Haley well saw the conflict of her both wanting people to "do it now" and "do it right." The description in DISC of this combination is called The Creative Pattern.

Chapter 3
CALL TO ADVENTURE

HEROINE'S JOURNEY

Life went on! A few months later, Moira reached out to invite Haley to join the "Take the Leap for Success" women's group coaching program that was scheduled to start in the new year. Haley was intrigued and looked forward to the possibility of meeting new people, so she signed up.

On the first night, Moira shared the Heroine's Journey of stepping into the unknown, using Dorothy from *The Wizard of Oz* as a classic example. There are times when change is thrust on someone, for example, the twister in the story. For many people it can be a health event, like it was for Audrey. For others, it could be a financial reversal or job loss, which Haley had experienced several times in her life with Clint as his career progressed. She recognized that she was being called to an adventure, the classic Heroine's Journey.

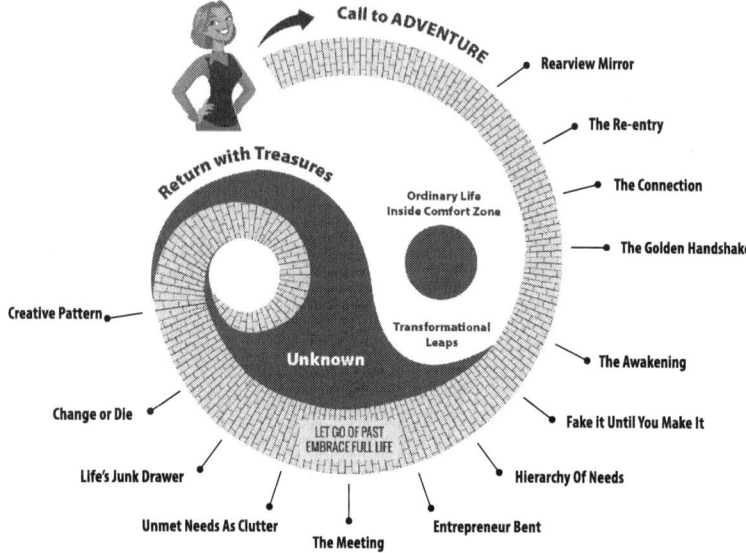

Haley's Heroine's Journey

Call to ADVENTURE

Rearview Mirror

The Re-entry

The Connection

The Golden Handshake

Ordinary Life
Inside Comfort Zone

Return with Treasures

Creative Pattern

Transformational
Leaps

Unknown

The Awakening

Change or Die

Fake it Until You Make It

LET GO OF PAST
EMBRACE FULL LIFE

Life's Junk Drawer

Hierarchy Of Needs

Unmet Needs As Clutter

Entrepreneur Bent

The Meeting

Moira shared that a minority of people do not wait to be hit on the head by change like a 2 x 4. They recognize their discontent with the status quo, along with an inner knowledge that there is so much more, and choose to take action and embrace change. Either way, the call to adventure takes one from the known to the unknown and is the beginning of transformation. Haley reflected on how her life thus far had followed a Heroine's Journey.

THE CHANGE CURVE

As the death of the old ways of living take place, there is rebirth in the new ways of life. Moira counseled that people go through what is often described as the stages of grief. As one replaces old behaviors with new actions, denial can be strong. Often there is resistance to the change. In many cases, what one resists actually persists. She called this process the "Change Curve" and shared how to move through it in a faster and easier fashion.

In the beginning, Haley's head was spinning. Many of her behaviors were ingrained from childhood. These included her father's German work ethic and her mother's desire for everyone to be happy. Both of these characteristics worked well for Haley's professional life. She attributed the combination in large part to why she had achieved such a high level of success in a short period of time.

THE ONLY ONE STOPPING ME IS ME

It was an epiphany to Haley, though, that the only person stopping her was her. By playing small and holding back her true self, she was actually hurting herself. The sense of safety she craved from Maslow's Hierarchy was actually an illusion.

She reflected on the experience of a couple from church. The husband had begun a career in government after college, believing it to be safe. He came to the conclusion during a government shutdown, which happened when he was in middle age, that nothing is truly safe. There were no guarantees. To quote Helen Keller: "Security is mostly a superstition. Avoiding danger is no safer in the long run than outright exposure. The fearful are caught as often as the bold . . . life is a daring adventure or nothing."

RELEASE THE OLD WAYS

The burnout rate was high in Haley's profession, and she too was feeling the effects. At that point, she was in her late fifties and in better physical shape and health than most of her family. Her maternal grandmother lived to her early nineties, so Haley predicted she would live another thirty-five to forty years! She wondered if she could sustain the level of effort that she had been maintaining. Something needed to change or she needed to change—and fast!

During one session, Moira had everyone write on small pieces of paper everything that they wanted to release to the universe. This could be habits, limiting beliefs, behaviors, ways of thinking, people. Anything and everything that no longer served the creation of the life they wanted and were meant to live. That night, the group of ladies went outside and set the slips of paper on fire in a burning bowl.

The mini-ceremony felt freeing, for about one minute, and then the old feelings of not being good enough resurfaced for Haley. She shared with the group that it seemed that everything was so hard.

FAST, EASY, AND FUN

Although she prided herself and her team's ability to work with challenging clients, it was wearing her out. Moira proclaimed that not only can it be fast and easy, but it can be fun, too. A key aspect to the process was to be willing to ask for, receive, and accept help.

As an outward sign that she was open to the process, the next time she was at Staples® picking up office supplies, Haley purchased an "EASY"™ button and left it on her desk. It served as a reminder to ceremonially release the hard clients and accept with grace the easy ones. Haley knew, though, there was something more in store for her.

CREATIVE, RESOURCEFUL, AND WHOLE

To move forward with the life she was designed to live also meant letting go of worrying about outcomes and the expectations of others. Many people use the analogy of air travel, when the flight attendant reminds passengers to put on their own oxygen masks first, before helping others near them. This is key to survival in air travel. Moira's message for life went beyond survival, to thrival. She shared that people are naturally creative, resourceful, and whole.

When people are released to become all that they can be, everyone benefits. Haley saw that her over-responsibility could potentially suffocate those around her. The easiest way for her to pivot her naturally critical perspective was to access curiosity. How could she see the person as creative, resourceful, and whole? It turned out that miracles abound and are only a thought away.

ENOUGH!

One of the challenges that Haley experienced as she began to make changes in her personal life was that she found that certain patterns were deeply ingrained. Many of the behaviors actually benefited her and others and led to her success. The inner critic kept her in perfectionist mode and assured that everything she did was at a high level of performance. This saboteur kept her in a constant state of feeling beaten down, like she wasn't enough.

A technique that she employed was to argue with her inner critic. Many times it felt as if she was negotiating against a top-level prosecuting attorney. Her emotional health was the pawn in these battles and the crazy thing was that it was not helpful. Why did she continue to do it and then expect a different outcome?

Moira suggested that rather than getting into an argument, to talk with her inner critic as though she was a small child in need of assurance. To promise her four-year-old self that she heard her and understood her feelings and knew they were real. Then she would put her hands on her heart and say affirming words, such as, "I unconditionally love and accept myself." These small steps began to break the cycle.

THE BIG LEAP

An avid book lover since childhood, Haley was reading *The Big Leap* by Gay Hendricks, a psychologist, writer, and teacher in the field of personal growth. Hendricks found that many people don't believe they deserve to be happy all the time, so unconsciously they capped their level of joy. Most people lived lives of quiet desperation.

People artificially limited their happiness, even going so far as to self-sabotage because they don't believe they deserve to have it all. He refers to this phenomenon as an upper-limit problem.

This resonated with Haley, perhaps because of her father's German heritage to always prepare for the worst, just in case. He believed that if things were going well, it would be seemingly inevitable that an undesirable event was just around the corner.

THE OTHER SHOE

Moira shared that it is possible that the other shoe to drop could be positive, to use curiosity as a positive alternative to critical and catastrophic thinking. She shared a poem by her friend Tammy Holland, entitled appropriately "Other Shoe to Drop." The message of the prose is there is beauty in considering all possibilities, both the good and those that may be perceived as bad at the time. And "what if" the other shoe does drop? Haley had proven her resilience under challenging circumstances. In all situations, she could either learn, grow, or become better than before.

Other Shoe to Drop

By Tammy Holland

I sit, waiting for the other shoe to drop.
Will today be the day?
Don't dare to get your hopes up. Today could be the day the
other shoe drops.

So what?
So what?
So what if the other shoe drops?

There are shoes dropping all around, but I only see the heavy,
Burdensome, oppressive ones.

I stumble upon another pile of shoes today.
There is beauty in the pile.
Shoes landing with a soft thud, dropped by a lover.
Shoes piled in a messy heap when friends gather.
Glass slippers lovingly discarded to the back of the closet
after an enchanting night.
Shoes kicked off at the back door, bigger over the years.
The kids are home safe.

There is beauty in the other shoe dropping.
Beauty all around.
It comes from within.
Waiting with anticipation for the other shoe to drop.

Fear and self-sabotage were the two most common ceilings that Haley realized she needed to break through. Hendricks called this an upper-limit mindset and, as a result, people create fake drama and unnecessary problems.

UPPER LIMITS

A common upper-limit mindset is fear. There's a famous quote by Marianne Williamson that our worst fear is not of failure, but "that we are powerful beyond measure." It rang true for Haley. If she knew and accepted that she had everything she needed to live up to her potential, that left her with no excuse not to.

Haley realized that the Zone of Genius was where she should strive to live. In real estate, appraisers talked about the value of property when it was at its highest and best use. Land could be used for a dump or for a park, for a commercial building or for a thriving school. Haley knew what it felt like when she was at her "highest and best self," what others called "flow." Time just seemed to fly by when she was in that state.

Haley's Heroine's Journey

Call to ADVENTURE

Return with Treasures

Ordinary Life
Inside Comfort Zone

Transformational
Leaps

Unknown

LET GO OF PAST
EMBRACE FULL LIFE

The Only One Stopping Me Is Me

Release The Old Ways

Fast, Easy & Fun

Enough!

The Big Leap

The Other Shoe

Upper Limits

Time Warps

The Deep Dive

Light-Bulb Moment

Big Magic Epiphany

Quantum Leap

Luck... Good? Bad?

Chapter 4
SHATTERING LIMITING BELIEFS

TIME WARPS

The idea of the passage of time being a matter of perspective led her to do more reading, which led her to Einstein. To paraphrase the famous theoretical physicist and inventor: One minute on a hot stove, or doing something you don't want to do, like sitting in traffic or a boring meeting, seems like eternity. One hour spent doing something meaningful that you are passionate about or with someone you love, and time flies by.

It depended on her perception of the activity. One was the perspective of abundance. The other was the perspective of scarcity.

Yet, Haley realized that she tended to fill up her hours and days with things she didn't really want to do or care that much about doing, crowding out and taking up the space for what really did matter. She said she wanted the time to do something meaningful and yet why didn't she? The concept that time was relative was another seed planted in Haley's subconscious.

PAINT NITE® NOVICE

Haley considered her strengths to be left-brain oriented, logical, analytical, and objective. Moira encouraged "right-brain"-oriented oriented activities of being curious, intuitive, and subjective.

Invited by friends to her first Paint Nite®, Haley resisted, sharing that she had never been creative. This self-concept came from her childhood, when she was pulled out of art classes in elementary school to attend speech therapy to correct an impediment.

Haley brought in her Paint Nite® "masterpiece" to share with the ladies' coaching group. By reflex, she immediately told the old story of her lack of creativity. Moira gently reflected back to Haley the critical words that she had just used to describe herself.

It was a pivotal moment, as Haley realized how judgmental her inner critic was and the considerable damage the negative self-talk was doing to her spirit. It illustrated how far Haley still had to go to unconditionally love and accept herself. Clint reminded her that she didn't get where she was in her fifties overnight and to allow time and space for change to happen.

INTENTION SETTING

Looking back at one of the intention-setting exercises early in the coaching program, Haley recalled that her first intention was to be "nonjudgmental." That word in itself spoke volumes as to where Haley's mindset was. Her inner voice was like a leading prosecuting attorney and she was the one on trial.

Soon, though, she was able to consider positive-oriented intentions such as being open, curious, mindful, with a sense of wonder and fully present.

The habits and mindsets from the past were strongly entrenched, as they had developed over many years. Bit by bit, though, Haley saw that she was breaking away and creating new neural pathways that led to positive self-talk and action.

The words of Deepak Chopra rang true for Haley: "Every time you are tempted to react in the same old way, ask if you want to be a prisoner of the past or a pioneer of the future." Truly, the Heroine's Journey of transformation was taking place as Haley let go of the old behaviors and committed daily to living a full life.

A NEW VISION

At her mother's eightieth birthday party, Haley caught a potential vision of her future self. The Fuller family was well known for their love of food—hence the slogan "Fill 'er up on Fuller Famous BBQ." Her mother, Rosemary, was just a quarter century older than her, and yet she walked with a cane for stability and she seemed to be shrinking, predominantly due to the curve in her back.

Haley had an epiphany that she truly was her own best asset. Her strongest ability was to create value and opportunity, to produce results that would impact and improve people's lives. That required her to have energy in order to be at her best.

Upon returning home, Haley immediately contacted a friend who had sent her a flyer about her personal training services. Sarah made openings in her schedule for Haley to train with her twice per week.

These two appointments were to be nonnegotiable, as Haley's vision for eighty was to be fit and trim. So that she could live a long, full, and healthy life. She shared the news with Clint. He was a bit concerned about the budget until Haley reminded him that his favorite Oracle from Omaha, Warren Buffett, proclaimed: "Ultimately, there's one investment that supersedes all others: yourself."

THE DEEP DIVE

In the fall of that year, Moira hosted a weekend retreat known as a "Deep Dive" at her mountain cabin. Each participant was to select one area that she wanted to explore in more detail and discover how to manifest it in her life. The objective was to leave from that weekend with an action plan with next steps for implementation.

There would be time for hiking, time by the outdoor fire pit, good food, and conversation with friends. The small group of women included Jenny and Lizzy.

Jenny used to own a catering business, which she sold to help her husband with his real estate business. Jenny's vision was to create a cooking school where people could learn to set up their kitchen for success and discover the joy she experienced when sharing her gift of food and hospitality.

Lizzy's passion was movement by yoga, and she wanted to set up programs in the schools, particularly with little ones. She saw how her young family benefited from a solid yoga practice and visualized a niche where she could expand it, starting at the preschool level.

Haley was still thinking about writing a book, which she talked about whenever people inquired about her passions. It occurred to her that it had been one year since she and Moira had first met for coffee, and she was no further along. It seemed she never had time to actually write. That wasn't so unusual; many people have been there. Perhaps you have had that experience, too.

TIME AND MONEY CONUNDRUM

It was that conundrum again of there not being enough time or money. The need was still strong for her to produce income at a high level in her profession in order to contribute to her and Clint's retirement reserves. Although both kids were out of college and launched, Clint was fast approaching sixty-five, and they didn't know how much longer he would be working. As Haley was seven years younger and in a profession where many chose to work well past the typical retirement age, she planned to give it another ten strong years before passing the baton to Anne.

THE COVER STORY

One of the exercises that Moira had the ladies complete over the weekend was to create a "cover story" of their idea. Each was to visualize their idea on the cover of a magazine.

Haley selected *Success* magazine and created the headline: "Haley Beck Book Blockbuster." She visualized the magazine featuring quotes from real estate guru Barbara Corcoran from *Shark Tank*, financial guru Suze Orman and, of course, her own partner, Anne Crawford. There were illustrations and sidebars about the theme of her book. For the first time, Haley actually could see her book come to life.

THE LIGHT-BULB MOMENT

Over the weekend, the ladies bonded over the activities Moira planned, interspersed with recreation, relaxation, healthy food prepared by Jenny, and time in nature. As the weekend wrapped up on Sunday afternoon, Moira had each of them spend time writing in their journals about what was stopping them from achieving their vision. Afterwards, each shared their thoughts with the others.

At that moment, Haley had an epiphany. The only thing truly stopping her from achieving her vision for her life, from doing what she said she wanted to do, was herself. Everything else was really an excuse. It was such a powerful moment. Even years later, the ladies and Moira continued to talk about how they "saw" the light bulb go on in Haley's mind.

Haley realized that it wasn't really about the time. It was about her belief that spending time on herself was selfish. Unless the activity was directly producing business or met family obligations, she felt like she shouldn't make it a priority.

THE COMMITMENT

Haley committed to the group to go back and share with her husband, Clint, her business partner, Anne, and their staff and team her passion to write a book. She asked for their support, which they granted wholeheartedly.

The time quandary once again reared its ugly head. At that juncture in her professional life, she was busy in spades. Little did she know, but a couple other epiphanies were right around the corner. Always one to share quotes to motivate her team, she affirmed herself with the words of Paulo Coelho: "And, when you want something, all the universe conspires in helping you to achieve it."

BIG MAGIC EPIPHANY

The next weekend, she had plans to travel to Dallas to visit with some college friends for a mini-reunion. She stayed with Missy and Bob, who had an amazing screened-in porch, where Haley visualized herself writing her book on her laptop. Haley had long ago made a personal commitment to herself to not work on plane rides; that time was reserved for reading. She had brought along the book *Big Magic* by Elizabeth Gilbert.

Haley remembered vividly that this was the place and time she experienced her second epiphany. In the book, Gilbert talked about how ideas float around in the universe and when an idea came to someone, it was their opportunity to take it and act on it. If that person chose not to, the reason didn't really matter; if the time had come for the idea to be present in the world, then the inspiration would find someone who would bring it to fruition. Ideas came from everywhere! Success went to those creators who harnessed and channeled the energy.

Being busy, claiming that one does not have enough time, was the most classic excuse people gave for the resistance to not act on inspiration. At that moment, Haley recognized that not only did she need to write her book, but that she needed to do it NOW before someone else did.

There had been several ideas and inventions she visualized in her mind through the years that she didn't act on. For example, she recalled that when Will was little and had a serious sensitivity to mosquito bites, it would be great to have a net with elastic edges for her to fit over the stroller to protect him. When later she saw her inspiration in a store, created by someone else, she experienced a sense of regret over the missed opportunity. Disappointment had taken a toll on her psyche. Not this time!

She was empowered by the words of Jim Rohn, American entrepreneur, author, and motivational speaker: "Time has more value than money. You can get more money, but you cannot get more time."

HOW TO MAKE TIME

The next epiphany came from the book *Better Than Before* by Gretchen Rubin. To write the *Happiness Project*, Rubin interviewed people about what would make them happy. She discovered that many people felt that pursuing happiness to be elusive. Most felt that they would be happy "when" they got a new job, lost ten pounds, traveled, or pursued hobbies. The interesting point of it was that if people knew what would make them happy, then why didn't they just do it?

Author and motivational speaker Wayne Dyer has said, "There is no way to happiness. Happiness is the way." Rubin believed that better habits held the key so that people could achieve the happiness they longed for. These strategies would better equip them to realize their dreams.

One idea from the book stood out to Haley. It involved using the one-hour "fall back" that occurred during Daylight Savings Time in the fall. This time effect gave everyone who lived in DST an "extra" hour. One's body was already programmed to get up an hour earlier. The idea was to capture that time. In the words of James Clear, habits expert and author of *Atomic Habits:* "It is better to make small progress every day than to do as much as humanly possible in one day." Do things you can sustain.

That's what Haley did. This was Haley's third epiphany: that if time was a human construct, then it meant that she actually had control over it. Haley found that investing the time in writing by doing it first thing in the morning was a powerful habit. She discovered that this was one of the keys to success for many writers—that it wasn't magic at all.

Chapter 5
EPIPHANIES

THE POWER OF THE TRILOGY OF EPIPHANIES

Once she "found" the time and made the commitment, the words began to flow onto the page. Haley realized the power of making time for creativity. What one focused on expands. As she focused on activities that were meaningful, self-actualizing, and fed her soul, it had a positive effect on other areas of her life.

DUE DILIGENCE

In Haley's experience in business and life, "success leaves clues." To connect and learn from people who had gone before in whatever area or field she was interested in pursuing had had a compound effect in her life so far. One of her objectives was to visit with other authors.

A few years back, a lender colleague hosted a seminar in partnership with a settlement firm that brought in the speaker Karen Briscoe, author of *Real Estate Success in 5 Minutes a Day*. As Karen was on the East Coast, they agreed to visit by Skype.

Karen agreed to introduce Haley to Hal Elrod, the author of the *Miracle Morning* series. She shared how personally meeting Hal led her to create a writing routine as part of her Miracle Morning practice. This helped her achieve a higher level of success as an author. She went on to share that she hosted the **5 Minute Success** podcast focused on her book concept and invited Haley to be a guest once her book was published.

QUANTUM LEAP

Hal encouraged Haley to attend the Best Year Ever Blueprint (BYEB) in December that was led with his business partner, Jon Berghoff. Affectionately known as BYEB, it was one of the most inspirational events she had ever attended.

Haley had participated in industry mastermind groups for a number of years and found them valuable in the early years. The focus of those events was primarily on productivity, which she could do with her eyes closed. She found that her opportunities exploded and her business expanded as she got outside her comfort zone. Haley was ready at this stage of her life to make self-actualization and personal development a priority.

The next level beyond BYEB was to join the year-long Quantum Leap Mastermind (QLM) program. The fees were more than she had ever spent. The good news was that Haley quickly made the decision to invest in herself. The mastermind group included entrepreneurs, speakers, coaches, sales professionals, authors, and top producers across many industries.

The QLM retreats, which were held in Austin and Cleveland each year, along with check-ins with her small group, propelled Haley to new levels of success in her business and life. Hal and Jon came from a place of generosity in their own lives and business, which attracted like-minded people. Truly, the secret to living was giving. The interactions and connections proved to be powerful, and she grew beyond her mind's conception.

MINI-SABBATICAL

It wasn't all smooth sailing, as life continued to happen. The financial market crash of 2008 and subsequent real estate correction led Congress to pass the Dodd-Frank Act. The second half of the legislation was implemented in October 2015, the same month that Haley finally made the commitment to write her book. That year, to date, had been one of her best years ever, so she saw it as an opportunity to take a mini-sabbatical.

What happened, though, was a much larger financial impact than she and many other lenders had anticipated. Haley's personal production went from closing five loans per week to one loan per week, a reduction of 80 percent. This was due in large part to the newly established Consumer Financial Protection Bureau, which was merged with the 1974 established Housing and Urban Development (HUD). This legislation, in Haley's view, effectively shut down lending while the banks and mortgage, settlement, and title firms reconfigured all the programs and protocols for loan approvals and closings.

LUCK. GOOD? BAD?

At the same time, Clint had a setback in his career as a CEO when a lawsuit that his firm was involved in did not turn out as favorably as the attorneys on the case had projected to the board. Clint was asked to "retire" early, as he was approaching sixty-five.

This meant that Haley became the primary breadwinner and caused her to seriously revaluate whether she should once again put her dreams on hold to focus on building her production back up.

The afternoon that Clint shared the news, Haley called Moira in a panic. The life she had been working so hard to create was now shattered. Moira shared the Buddhist message about how what is perceived as adversity can turn out to be a blessing. Perhaps you have heard the story?

> *There is a Taoist story of an old farmer who had worked his crops for many years. One day, his horse ran away. Upon hearing the news, his neighbors came to visit. "Such bad luck," they said sympathetically.*

"Maybe," the farmer replied.

The next morning the horse returned, bringing with it three other wild horses. "How wonderful," the neighbors exclaimed.

"Maybe," replied the old man.

The following day, his son tried to ride one of the untamed horses, was thrown, and broke his leg. The neighbors again came to offer their sympathy on his misfortune.

"Maybe," answered the farmer.

The day after, military officials came to the village to draft young men into the army. Seeing that the son's leg was broken, they passed him by. The neighbors congratulated the farmer on how well things had turned out.

"Maybe," said the farmer.

TIME OUT

And yet, Haley felt busier than ever. It seemed as though busy had become a badge of honor. The people in her life also wanted to proclaim how "busy" their lives were. Busy had become a competitive arena; it somehow proclaimed importance. When she would ask someone, "How are you?" they often answered, "Good, but busy." She herself was guilty of this, as she recalled saying those exact words recently when visiting with a friend after church.

"Busy" meant that she had a lot going on, that she was in demand. And yet, although it felt like society had gotten faster and busier and this was a modern problem, it was actually age-old. More than 2,500 years ago, the ancient Chinese philosopher Lao Tzu said: "Time is a created thing." To say "I don't have time" is like saying, "I don't want to."

Haley realized busy meant she didn't have to change. It was safe: she could stay where she was used to being—in her comfort zone.

But, busy had a cost. It could close off her time for creativity, personal development, self-care, relationships, and opportunities.

After all, time was a nonrenewable resource.

Once that second and minute and hour and day and week and year were gone, she knew she could never get them back. Time poverty was epidemic. There would never be enough time to do something she didn't want to do. Most people didn't burn out—they timed out. Thirteenth-century Persian poet Rumi said: "Happiness is now."

What if Haley flipped the pyramid in her own life and started with self-actualization? Self-actualization meant achieving her full potential, everything she was capable of becoming. What did self-actualization look like? What was her highest and best self?

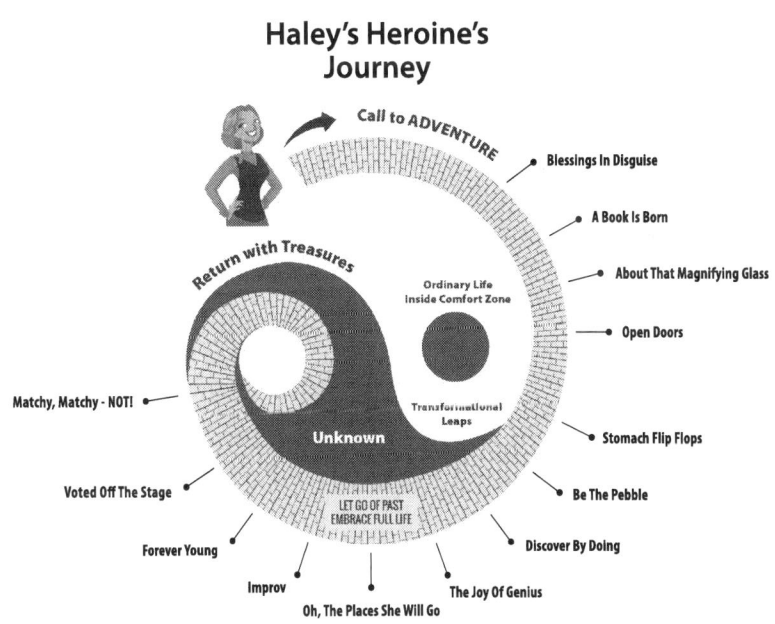

Chapter 6
BLESSED ASSURANCE

BLESSING IN DISGUISE

Clint's unscheduled retirement did prove to be a blessing, although not right away, as often is the case. One of the affirmations Haley learned from Hal Elrod became her mantra during this period: "There is nothing to fear, because you cannot fail—only learn, grow, and become better than you've ever been before." Haley focused on that paradigm shift in her thinking. She persisted in writing the book, while at the same time she double-timed her lead-generation efforts.

Soon she was back on track and very busy. Clint did some consulting in his industry and played golf and fished more. He was accustomed to living a fuller life, which included going to an office every day. After a few months, he asked Haley how he could help with her business. That led to Clint earning his license as a mortgage broker, and over time he became a valuable member of the team.

The idea of putting oneself first may seem counterintuitive. Haley reflected that many are taught that they should put others first, herself included. What she found is that personal development and self-actualization can have a positive impact on those around her. She recalled a quote from Shakespeare, an English poet and playwright: "Nothing is either good or bad except your thinking makes it so."

A BOOK IS BORN

The book was ready for sale on Amazon and other sites on August 1. Haley remembers the day vividly, as it felt to her like giving birth. From conception to delivery, the time frame was nine months. The process included hundreds of hours of writing, several rounds with the editor, many consultations with the cover and layout designer and countless emails, meetings, and phone calls with the publisher.

Much like when she gave birth to Will and Mattie, Haley was exhausted. She soon woke up to the realization that the "real work" was just beginning. The raising of children is an effort that spans their lifetime, and she quickly concluded it to be similar with book publishing.

BECOMING REAL

To launch a book for sale is just the beginning; the promotion is ongoing. Will purchased her first book on Amazon and had the date stamp on the back to prove it! This still brings a smile to Haley's face, basking in the support of her family.

She recalled the children's book *The Velveteen Rabbit*, by British author Margery Williams, that she read to her kids when they were young. In the story, the rabbit became "real" from the boy's love. After all those years of talking about it, her book became real. Truly it was a labor of love.

BE, DO, HAVE

The BE, DO, HAVE framework is known throughout the thought world of inspirational and motivational literature. Haley was first exposed to it by Moira, who found that as an executive and life coach, when people get the "order" in priority, everything else falls into place. The primary reason is that it becomes part of one's identity.

This made Haley think of one of her favorite movies, *The Bucket List*. In it two elderly men, auto mechanic Carter Chambers (Morgan Freeman) and hospital-corporation head Edward Cole (Jack Nicholson), happened to share the same hospital room. Life became more precious when diagnosed with terminal cancer.

The men commit to each other to fulfill their personal desires through "The Bucket List" before they "kick the bucket." Cole, a very successful businessman, funds the travel and activities components of the list, which included: witness something truly majestic, help a complete stranger, laugh until they cried, drive a Shelby Mustang, kiss the most beautiful girl in the world, get a tattoo, go skydiving, visit Stonehenge, drive a motorcycle on the Great Wall of China, go on a Safari, visit the Taj Mahal, sit on the Great Egyptian Pyramids, and find the joy in life.

It means, for example, that if you want to have the lifestyle of a wealthy person, you must first become that person before you can possess the wealth. Part of the reason most people fail is that they believe it is the other way around.

One of the items Carter talks about is Mt. Everest in the Himalayas, referring to it in the movie as "my mountain." On the actual bucket list, he writes *Witness Something Truly Majestic*. Apparently, he just wanted to see the thing, but when they got close were told that they could not do a fly-over because of a storm on the mountain. That's the "shitty news"; the "really shitty news" is that the weather won't clear till spring.

To check off the experience on the ultimate life list would bring happiness. What happened when the view is obstructed by bad weather? Cole attempted to be philosophical and said that perhaps the mountain was trying to tell Carter something, to which Carter said, perhaps it means it is time to go home. Is the experience no longer meaningful? What happens to one's purpose when weather, health, and circumstances don't cooperate?

Haley learned that a way to reframe this situation in the BE, DO, HAVE perspective was to set the intention to BE happy and to be present no matter the outcome; this led to DO the experience and in the moment to HAVE meaning in BEING there. At the conclusion of the movie, after both men have passed away, the assistant fulfilled their wish by leaving their ashes at the top of the mountain. In a way, then they were always present for the view!

Many people, it seems, desire to HAVE money and so they DO work in order to BE happy. The paradigm shift for Haley was to BE happy as her true self-actualized self and DO meaningful work so that she would HAVE prosperity.

This paradigm shift exploded in Haley's mind. Her success in life so far was in large part the result of Doing! She was an expert in productivity, which led to recognition, accomplishments, and possessions. As many others who have gone before, she felt that there was still so much more. She committed to BE first, then to DO the behavior, and then she would HAVE her heart's desire.

ABOUT THAT MAGNIFYING GLASS!

What one focuses on expands! For Haley, this concept was key to "Appreciative Inquiry," which was discovering what works best, gives life, creates energy and excitement, and then seeks to create more of that which is good. Jon Berghoff utilized the concept, developed by David Cooperrrider, PhD on the retreats with the QLM community at the individual and group levels.

These ideas were the opposite direction from Haley's background, where it was drilled into her that every mistake and action should be analyzed to determine what went wrong. No wonder she felt like she was always on trial! What a fresh perspective to put energy into positive thought and actions to create a compelling vision for the future.

OPEN DOORS

One of Haley's favorite quotes was by inventor Alexander Graham Bell: "Sometimes we stare so long at a door that is closing that we see too late the one that is open."

To get her message out to the marketplace, Haley spoke at local mortgage and real estate offices and held "lunch and learns" in conjunction with title company representatives. It was the Hal Elrod mastermind community that truly rallied around her. The members of the community wrote reviews on Amazon, shared on Facebook, and posted on social media sites, along with making key introductions to influencers and podcast hosts. A friend in the title business included her book as part of a review on **Inman News**, a leading source for real estate news, technology, mortgage, commentary, and events. That one review drove her book to the bestseller category on Amazon.

THE GREAT DEBATE

A debate going on in Haley's mind was whether to produce an audio version of the book. The wisdom of sales guru Zig Ziglar, to use time in her car as an "automobile university," rang true. With modern technology, it was easier than ever to turn daily tasks like walking the dog and making coffee into learning time with audiobooks and podcasts. She felt intuitively that this was the future of publishing content.

On the other hand, after surviving the Great Recession by being mindful of expenses, she was hesitant to invest additional resources into the book until it had proven itself. Preliminary costs for talent and production were considerably higher than anticipated.

Haley posed the dilemma to her mastermind small group when it was her turn to be in the "hot seat." The idea to reach to out to fellow QLM member Julie Reisler was suggested. Julie had recently published her own book and personally recorded the audio. Turned out, Julie's talents were multifaceted, including being a life designer and coach. Once the connection was made, Julie was "all in." Over time, audio sales for Haley's books considerably surpassed the print and digital versions. Haley recognized another situation where the stumbling block was mostly in her own mind.

BIRTHDAY GIFT

It was on webinars, podcasts, and Facebook live events that Haley found that she made the most impact. The medium offered the strongest reach and meant she could keep travel for recreation, relaxation, and to see the world. To do this, Haley set up a "studio" in her office, complete with a Blue Yeti microphone and professional headset.

The book opened countless doors and opportunities that Haley could not have been able to visualize just a few years before. On the first anniversary of her book, the team hosted a birthday party and countless people sent in videos with well wishes.

To keep with the theme, people asked what her book wanted for its first birthday and all of sudden it became clear: it should have a podcast. She once again reached out to Karen Briscoe, the host of the *5 Minute Success* podcast, which had achieved the rank of the number-one most recommended business podcast in its novice year. If she could do it, then maybe Haley could too!

Chapter 7
IF SHE CAN DO IT, SO CAN I!

THE PODCAST

Karen was generous with her time and knowledge. She truly did "pay it forward" and shared with Haley all the lessons learned and tips she wished she had known when she decided to launch the *5 Minute Success* podcast. And, best of all, Karen invited Haley to be a guest on the highly ranked *5 Minute Success* show. Haley's podcast would continue the message in her book.

The show would feature interviews with people who were on the Heroine's and Hero's Journey to live a full life of self-actualization. One of the amazing outcomes of the podcast was being able to interview people who Haley admired. In many cases, she would not have been in a position to have a one-on-one with these famous authors, speakers, coaches, entrepreneurs, business owners, and thought-leaders otherwise. She was truly creating the life of her dreams in real time!

Each conversation caused her to make time to reflect on her own journey into the unknown. That first flip made all the difference, as Haley recalled Lao-Tzu's timeless message: *A journey of a thousand miles begins with a single step*. To travel that journey required the next step and the next step, which Haley saw as flips.

STOMACH FLIP-FLOPS

There were still flips going on in her stomach, though, because launching a podcast is quite an endeavor. What if no one listened? What if her speech impediment came back and she slurred her words? What if no one cared and it flopped?

There was the imposter syndrome rearing its ugly head again. The theatre of voices in her mind was so loud! Who was she to think she could host a podcast? Where was she going to get the time! Haley reflected on how far she had come. What surprised her is that she felt she still had to prove that she was worthy of investment of time and money into her ideas.

When she first learned about the "Change Curve" from Moira in the coaching program, it seemed like her progress was two steps forward and one step back. Moira called that the "Frankenstein Walk." Whenever someone ventured into the known, that feeling and experience was to be considered normal and expected.

Haley immediately recognized that she was not in mortal danger, so she could breeze through the denial stage. She was clearly stuck in resistance once again. Her confidence in her entrepreneurial ability was strong, as she had proven success in starting other endeavors and businesses. What surprised her was that she felt she still had to prove that she was worthy of the investment of time and money into her ideas.

She was compassionate with her scared younger self that had a speech impediment. She was curious with appreciative inquiry questions. What if she could do it? What if she was a success? What if she could impact and improve more lives? And then she was courageous, and she quickly took action. It was fast, easy and fun.

CREATIVE ENDEAVORS

The only way for the creator to know herself was to create. What one focused on expanded. As she began to experience the benefits of being creative, she wanted to do more. The length of life was finite, but it's width and depth depended on each person to determine.

Time expanded when Haley was living in her zone of genius. Previously, when Haley rationalized why she shouldn't or couldn't take time or make time or create time for her creative side, she recognized them for the rational lies that were the basis of the negative self-talk.

BE THE PEBBLE

This time around, Haley was quicker to affirm her value and worth to herself. After all, her family, staff and team, clients, and the broader community all benefited from her previous ventures.

At the first BYEB Haley attended, one of the activities was to discuss well-known proverbs and then to create a "new" one. Her small group talked about what it meant to change the world and the proverb of the ripple effect that was created when one threw a pebble into a body of water. The "new" proverb Haley proposed was: Be the pebble that causes the ripple.

The ripple effect of her focus on self-actualization actually improved the lives of the people around her! She reflected on all the jobs and opportunities her ideas created. She found that what was good for her often was better for other people. It wasn't selfish at all, as was her belief system for so many years. What's good for her could actually be BETTER for those around her.

IT'S ABOUT TIME

Haley's concept was an idea whose "time had come." The universe gave her the idea and it was hers to implement. And she was finding it to be fast, easy, and fun—just as Moira had shared at the first ladies group coaching session.

This proved to be another BE, DO, HAVE shift. To BE the pebble meant for Haley to actively live as her highest and best self. This meant she would DO creative, meaningful and valuable work. And this, in fact, meant that she and others would HAVE prosperity.

DISCOVER BY DOING

Once Haley was in the exploration stage of the "Change Curve," she felt more confident. By getting into action, the motion created the energy to discover by doing. Getting curious created the energy to figure out how to make it happen.

A couple of friends from the QLM had podcasts, so she reached out to them. Those conversations empowered her to commit to take the baby steps to make it happen. She found that life proceeded in line with her intentions for it.

WHAT'S YOUR STATE?

Haley was a fan of American life coach, author, and entrepreneur Tony Robbins, who referred to setting intentions as one's state. One always had a choice. It came from the idea from that one's energy in a state affected how that situation turned out.

Haley found that establishing her intended state was a pivotal moment. Before doing anything, she now reflected on whether she had set the right intention to accomplish her purpose. This led, in many cases, to the creation of optimal experiences.

All of a sudden, Haley realized that she was in the final stage of the "Change Curve." One of Haley's natural strengths and abilities was the implementation and integration of systems and leverage. Once those were in place, the podcast was in launch mode.

The first hundred episodes included greats such as Hal Elrod, author of the *Miracle Morning* series; Karen Briscoe of *5 Minute Success*; Gay Hendricks, author of *The Big Leap* and countless other books; Jaime Masters of *Eventual Millionaire*; and Jay Papasan of *The One Thing*.

THE JOY OF GENIUS

As she began to experience the taste of success—the "Joy of Genius" as Gay Hendricks refers to it in *The Big Leap*—she was able to see how she was also moving more quickly through the change curve. She began to anticipate the change rather than waiting for it to hit her with a 2 x 4. This reminded her of a quote by the famous hockey player, Wayne Gretzky, that he was successful because he skated where the puck was going.

BLAH, BLAH, BLAH

One of the key aspects of Haley's Miracle Morning routine included reciting affirmations. Unless she was proactive, negative talk seemed to be on continuous play in her head. It reminded her of the voices Charlie Brown heard in the Charles Schulz *Peanuts* cartoons. All adults sounded like "blah, blah, blah." Ongoing, purposeful effort via habit and routines were instrumental in making this paradigm shift for Haley. BE became to Haley what her life was like "before epiphany" and AE was "after epiphany."

OH, THE PLACES SHE WILL GO

Haley kept a "life list" rather than a "bucket list," believing that her focus should be on living her fullest life now while she created and co-created the life of her dreams. Once Will and Mattie graduated from college and successfully launched their careers, the family had the resources to step up their travel schedule, particularly abroad.

It was quite an elaborate mix and match; every December the Beck family made plans about where to travel in the next year. The preference was for active travel in exotic places. Haley's love was hiking, Clint preferred biking, Mattie wanted kayaking, and Will loved anything high-adventure, including water sports, zip lining, rock climbing, and even camel riding. The family enjoyed an annual ski trip, as well as travels to Iceland, Ecuador, and the Galapagos Islands.

Life was full and good. Haley loved her life while she created and co-created the life of her dreams.

IMPROV

The podcast format allowed for each guest to bring to the recording their own story and style. For Haley, the most intellectually stimulating aspect of being a host was how best to respond to "whatever" the guest lobbed her way. She reflected on how far she had come in life. Just think, even a child with a speech impediment can become a podcast host. As a stretch goal for the year, she signed up for an Improv class.

The games played in Improv kept Haley on her toes. She had to pay close attention and focus in the skits to know how to respond to keep the thread going. "Yes, and" is one of the key premises of Improv and it quickly became Haley's favorite go-to response in other areas of her life.

Chapter 8
NO TIME LIKE THE PRESENT

FIFTY-NINE IS A VERY GOOD YEAR

The summer of her fifty-ninth year was especially full. In August, she was scheduled to be out of the office for the longest period of time ever in her career as a mortgage lender. First off was a trip to Peru with Will to hike the Inca Trail to Machu Picchu.

FOREVER YOUNG

The Peruvian train made a stop at #104 for the one-day Inca Trail hikers to embark on their journey to the Machu Picchu Sun Gate. Haley took in the incredible views along the journey. Lunch was at the famous Inca ruins known as "Forever Young." It seemed ironic in a way, that truly only those who are physically capable of the strenuous activity were the ones who could appreciate the experience. Haley realized that staying "forever young" was both physical and a state of mind.

The lyrics of Bob Dylan's song by the same name came to Haley as she hiked. She recalled the music of her youth, and it made her realize that she still has a song to sing.

> *May your heart always be joyful*
> *May your song always be sung*
> *And may you stay*
> *May you stay forever young*

STAIRMASTER

The final hike at Machu Picchu was to Punta Montana, a very vigorous vertical hike overlooking the famous ruin city. The entry was timed and passport-controlled. Haley had a photo of her and Will being "granted" access. Hikers must reach the summit by noon, or they will be instructed to proceed back down; for safety purposes, everyone must be off the mountain before dark.

The Stairmaster nature of the hike was apparent right at the start. Being in Peru, there were no hand or guard rails. The views were priceless, and on the way up Haley stopped at every turn to take photos. Not surprisingly, Will scampered like a goat way ahead of Haley. She just put one foot in front of the other.

IF ONLY

At what seemed like a little past the halfway mark, she met up with a couple from their group. Although older in age than Haley, they were from California, athletically inclined and fit. In fact, the day before, the husband was trail running the Inca with Will.

His wife said that the height was causing him to experience vertigo. His fear was about how he was going to get back down. These thoughts paralyzed him from moving forward. Haley said that she could understand how he might feel that way. She was focused on the top and having photos taken with Will. She moved on so that she would stay in a positive frame of mind.

Sharing the experience and views at the top with Will was worth it! The photos were priceless. Her fitness tracker said that she climbed the equivalent of 252 floors that day. To put this in perspective, a flight of stairs is counted as approximately ten feet of elevation gain, which are approximately sixteen steps. This was an extreme activity!

At dinner that night, she visited with the couple about the day. The man said that if only one of the guides had said to him that the view was worth it and that that he could do it, he would have had the confidence to go on. Haley reflected to herself, isn't that true about most of life?

VOTED OFF THE STAGE

Next up was the QLM in Cleveland. Prior to the retreat, everyone was to prepare a "TEDx"-style talk of about five minutes in length of an 'idea worth sharing." The participants would deliver their message to a small group. Each group would select one person to present to the entire community as the evening's entertainment.

It felt to Haley a little like the ***America's Got Talent***, a survivor-style reality U.S. television show. Although she prided herself on her strong, competitive nature, she felt intimidated by the process. Deep down, one of the secret desires of her heart was to be selected to present her talk at the BYEB in San Diego in December. Her understanding was that the people who "won" in Cleveland would be the lucky few.

PUNCH BUGGY

Haley chose to share a family story about when the new Volkswagen Beetle cars were introduced to the U.S. market. It was the summer of 2001, and Will and Mattie were in late and middle elementary, which meant for Haley lots of time in the minivan transporting kids around to activities. At the heart was a story of her personal worthiness, which meant she would need be at her most vulnerable.

The family had heard the story many times of how Haley owned an orange "retro" VW bug in college. It held many fond memories of her youth and freedom. On long drives to stave off boredom, whenever a VW bug would pass, they always played the "Punch Buggy" game.

At one of the sightings of a new bug, Haley shared with her family her dream to own one of the cars. In her fantasy life, it would be yellow, as that has always been her favorite color. A yellow VW is cheerful, youthful, and fun—the opposite of what Haley had felt with her current life of heavy responsibilities. Will was quick to proclaim that there was no way Dad would ever let her have a VW. Wow, those words hit Haley right between the eyes. She shot back that she was old enough to have any car she wanted.

MINIVAN PHASE OF LIFE

Will did not believe her, so quickly they got Clint on the phone. He started in on all the reasons a VW was impractical for their lives: they were still in the "minivan" phase of life with kids and gear to haul around; Clint was 6'4" and didn't think he could comfortably fit in a VW bug; they still had a loan balance on the minivan; and living on one income meant buying another car was not in the budget.

After each of these objections, Haley responded: "I hear you, but I am old enough to have any car I want." Finally Clint came around and reluctantly agreed that Haley was at an age to have any car she wanted.

With that, Haley was satisfied and said she really didn't "need" the car anymore. She just wanted Clint to recognize her inherent worth and that she was allowed to have dreams of her own. Now she just needed to be sure that Will and Mattie knew that too.

Haley was nervous sharing this story with the group, and it showed. Instead of hers, the group of six selected the powerful story of a woman who was a survivor of sexual abuse as a child and had gone on to thrive and was an author, coach, and speaker on the topic. Haley's inner critic went into overdrive, beating her up for sharing such a petty story. She put her inner critic in time out and took a walk to be good to herself for living outside her comfort zone.

CO-CREATE EPIPHANY

The last activity of the mastermind group was to share with another person one's plans upon returning home. Haley paired up with a young woman who was getting married in the next thirty days. The young soon-to-be bride was passionate about sharing her life with her fiancé and making plans together.

It hit Haley that the last few years she had been making plans for her future, which included Clint and her family, of course. What she hadn't ever really done was ask Clint about his vision for life. To go beyond solo creative endeavors, to co-create the life of their dreams together. That was a monumental wake-up call, which led to many meaningful conversations.

One of the most powerful Hal Elrod's affirmations for Haley, "Love the life you have while you create the life of your dreams" became for her "Love the life you have while you create and co-create the life of your dreams." Dreams really could and do come true and were more meaningful when shared.

THE BIG LEAP RETREAT

The other event in August of that year was a retreat hosted by Moira Lethbridge. The first retreat was "Take the Leap to Success" and this one was "The Big Leap." It was held at a farm with rolling hills, stunning sunsets, a pool, fire pit, and private chef, with amazing meals shared in the screened-in gazebo.

Haley was skeptical if she could comfortably be gone that long from her business, and yet she was committed to all three opportunities. She had experienced the epiphany that changed her life dramatically at Moira's first retreat; she was excited and a little anxious about what could possibly happen at this one.

It was a small group. Haley knew Christina best from being in group coaching together for about a year. Christina's passion was to create films, particularly documentaries, on issues that she felt were important for people to address. She had been in an area of film production early in her career and moved out of it to get into the more lucrative side of sales. Similar to many women who are in the throes of child-rearing years, she felt frustrated with life and came to coaching to get her passion back.

Haley was a bit stumped as to what her "next" was, as felt that she was already doing so much. That's when Christina blurted out, "I think that you should do a TEDx talk." Immediately Haley could hear her prosecuting attorney proclaim that idea was WAY out of her comfort zone, shouting out objections as to why that would not be possible. It was LOUD. The good news was that Haley also could hear the intuitive guide that whispered that she could and should do this. For once it was more compelling than her inner critic.

A seed was planted.

MATCHY, MATCHY—NOT

The Secret® by Rhonda Byrne—including the book, movie, and countless other motivational materials—made a tremendous impact on people's lives, including Haley's. It illustrated how the Law of Attraction was energy and that like attracted like. It teaches that to achieve one's vision, thoughts become actions, which lead to manifestation.

Haley had felt and continued to feel daily the power of wholehearted commitment. First she demonstrated it in her profession as a mortgage lender, next as an author, and then as a podcast host. What she discovered along the journey was that it wasn't always matchy, matchy. At times what she received was better than what she could even have imagined.

When obstacles appeared, she found it to be even more crucial to push through quickly. In the words of American writer, editor, and educator George Leonard: "Resistance is proportionate to the size and speed of the change, not to whether the change is a favorable or unfavorable one." What was the outcome for Haley? She "failed" forward more quickly; moved on to the "next" faster; or learned, grew, and became better than before. And sometimes she would enjoy the benefits of embracing the change.

Chapter 9
POSITIVE PEER PRESSURE

THE SETBACK

The Beck family was looking forward to September of that year, when a couple of Will's best friends, Heath and Emily, were getting married. The previous spring the gang was celebrating all together at a local Mexican restaurant. Over margaritas, they started talking about participating in the Boulder Sunset Triathlon two weeks prior to the wedding.

As Clint was going to be out of town, Emily encouraged Haley to join her on the Sprint, which is typically a half-mile swim, 12.5-mile bike ride, and 5k run. Haley blurted out that although she liked to bike and hike, she had never considered herself an athlete and had never participated in any athletic event.

The positive peer pressure was strong and overcame Haley's fear of failure, so she registered for the event with the group of thirty-somethings. As she trained over the summer at the club, she struggled with the idea of the open-water swim. Apparently that was the leg of the event that challenged many people mentally.

Haley visited with everyone she knew who had competed in triathlons, as was her practice when trying something new—and particularly when outside her comfort zone. Heath set up a practice open-water swim the Saturday morning before the Sunday race, which Haley aced. She was ready!

Haley was really disappointed when a severe summer thunderstorm came through the day of the scheduled race. She had psyched herself up for her first Sprint Tri and, with her training, she began to take on the identity of an athlete.

FAIL FORWARD

She would not, could not, let the setback hold her down for long. There were still a few Sprint Triathlons scheduled near Denver before the season closed down for winter. She signed up to compete in the first available event at nearby Loveland Lake.

By then it was mid-October and the temperature was brisk in the mornings. Haley consulted her triathlon friends and they all recommended she rent a wet suit just in case the water temperature was below the guideline level. So she did, and Clint took some hilarious photos of her as she squeezed herself into it! Although she didn't have the gang's encouragement the day of the race, she had Clint, her rock and main cheerleader.

THE WATER IS WARM!

The excitement of participants and spectators alike filled the air the morning of the race. The officials declared the water temperature warm enough that wet suits would not be permitted for those competing for medals. Haley was unsure whether to wear it. The air temperature was still cool and it was only her second time to complete an open water swim. What to do?!?

Clint suggested she check out the water temperature, so Haley set off to the edge of the lake. As she dipped her foot into the water, she commented to a nearby gentlemen that she didn't know what to do about the wet suit. He said that if she didn't need the wet suit, she shouldn't wear it. Haley inquired as to what he meant by "need it," and he clarified that wet suits offer buoyancy in addition to warmth.

She responded confidently that she did not "need" the wetsuit for buoyancy, only warmth. This wise stranger asked something of Haley that stayed with her the rest of her life: "Then why on earth would you disqualify yourself before you even get in the water?"

Haley shared that this was her very first triathlon, she was only doing the sprint, and she had never participated in any type of race before, ever. Basically she didn't consider herself an athlete, wasn't going to win anything, so why would it matter if she was disqualified? She was just doing the race to prove to herself and her kids that she could.

To this he said, "You don't know that, you might win something. The truth is that nobody ever won a game they didn't play." Truly, she was convinced. It seemed that even with as far as she had already traveled on her journey of self-actualization, Haley's inner critic was still strong. Crazy thing was, this time she spoke the words out loud and someone had the good sense to call her on it. She refocused her thoughts on those that affirm and empower and set out to compete in her first Tri! *Look out world*, she thought, *change is a-happening*!

LOGISTICS SETBACK

The swim leg was a breeze and Haley was glad she swam without the wet suit, as the temperature was comfortable without it. It was still chilly, though, so she grabbed her backpack with a change of clothes that she planned to wear for the bike and run portions. Her well-packed bag was missing a key item—her running bra! Clint was nearby to help with the logistics of changing in a porta-potty, and he said that she could bike without it.

Haley exclaimed, yes, she could. What about the run? she wondered out loud. That would be very uncomfortable and slow her down. Clint agreed to help locate a bra in their luggage so she could get on her bike and back into the race. It was obvious that very few people were stopping to change clothes! Most of the racers were just doing minor changes in the transition area.

This snafu meant another pit stop between the bike ride and run, which cost her time. Running across the finish line was truly a moment to remember. Clint captured a lot of photos, which made her "famous" on social media with friends and family.

THE NOVICE PLACES!

After all that exercise, Haley was starving, so they packed up and got on the road, planning to stop at a local Mexican restaurant they saw on their way to the lake. The race results were posted by then, so Haley checked them out. In the novice category, she was the oldest female to place! And if she had not lost all that time to changing clothes, TWICE, she imagined how much better she could do!

80 X 80 MOVEMENT

Clint shared his pride of her placement, and Haley basked in the glory of the accomplishment. The Fuller family was known for their great BBQ, not athletics, so this was all new to her. Many people asked if she would compete again, to which she replied, "Sure, I'm likely to be one of those crazy people who commit to complete eighty by the time I turn eighty."

And thus the 80 x 80 Movement was born! It was another "big magic" moment, when she realized that the universe had blessed her with an idea and it was hers to make happen. Known for getting into action quickly, Haley purchased the domain www.80x80Movement.com and set about bringing the idea to fruition.

BE, DO, HAVE

The **80 x 80 Movement - Challenges for Life - Milestones and Medals** was a life flip for Haley. One of the key perspective shift in the BE, DO, HAVE mindset framework had to do with her physical self.

The "before" Haley wanted to BE thin so she would DO diets and extreme exercise in which she found that she would HAVE limited success. This led to yo-yo weight and poor body self-image. The "after epiphany" Haley strived to BE her highest and best self, which led her to DO movement and eat well, so that she would HAVE health. The new paradigm came from a place of positive choice.

Chapter 10
WHAT'S NEXT?

THE NEXT

Since returning from the "The Big Leap" retreat in August, the question "but how" to get on a TEDx stage would run through Haley's mind. It was now several months later, and she had not made much progress. She knew a few people who had been on TEDx stages, and she set out to connect with them. That research led her to figure out basic logistics of when and where the next events took place and how to apply.

As often happens when Haley took action, it led to knocking over a string of dominos. A Facebook friend recommended she present her first talk at an "open mic speaker audition" event coming up in Colorado Springs on November 7. As an added bonus, this meant that she and Clint could stay at the Broadmoor, one of their favorite destination hotels. As it was already September 24, she felt the urgency created by establishing a hard deadline!

At this juncture, Haley had delivered numerous trainings to professionals in her industry. She had been a guest on countless media opportunities, such as webinars and podcasts. And she continued to host her own podcast twice a week.

What she found, though, was a standup presentation in front of an audience with no notes and PowerPoint as a crutch was a different situation altogether. This was another level of achievement in her knowledge, skills, and ability. From past experience, she recognized the benefit of working with a coach. Thus, she reached out to her network for recommendations.

Carol Cox, founder of Speaking Your Brand, a coach in Florida, came highly recommended as a professional who specialized in working with speakers to craft and deliver a signature talk. After an introductory call and viewing the videos for several speakers that Carol had coached to success, Haley committed to Carol's half-day Zoom call program, which they scheduled for October 26.

PARKINSON'S LAW

One of the key attributes of Haley's success was her ability to get results. This was achieved by setting a timeline with steps that became habits to accomplish her objectives. She found that time expanded or contracted based on the time allotted. It is similar to the phenomenon that people are the most productive right before leaving for vacation.

In Haley's research about habit formation, she discovered that this behavior was known as "Parkinson's Law." Limiting and restricting time can actually make people more efficient and effective. Once she understood the power behind the principles of the law, she applied it to other areas of her business and life, including the signature talk preparation.

When people would tell Haley that they don't have time, she would ask them: "Can you invest five minutes a day?" She told them that starting small and building up was a proven method of habit formation.

TIME STRETCHING

The timeline was aggressive! Haley sent Carol her remarks from the August QLM presentation, along with some thoughts on other topics of interest. The Zoom call session moved quickly, almost like a pinball machine. As ideas bounced around, Carol jotted them on Post-it notes in bright colors to create a storyboard. Once the line of the story thread was in place, the ladies crafted the talk in "real time." The plan was set for Haley to memorize the eight-minute presentation and send Carol videos for her input over the next ten days.

Carol advocated that a key to successful speaking delivery was to present in front of a live audience whenever possible. The team leader for her company arranged for several occasions for Haley to deliver the message in front of various groups. On one of the practice presentations, she froze. Her inner critic actually spoke out loud with a negative stream of comments. After a few deep breaths, she regained her composure and finished. She sent the mistakes and all to Carol, who gave her some tips and strategies on how to handle it if that should happen again in the future.

SIGNATURE TALK ON THE RED CARPET

Haley and Clint arrived a day early to the Broadmoor for recreation and rejuvenation. They made time for a vigorous hike in the refreshing, clear fall air. The next morning at the event check-in with the organizers, she was told that her talk was to be the last presentation prior to lunch.

The timing turned out to be beneficial, as by watching the speakers present before her, Haley gained confidence in her message and skills. All went well! In a way it was anticlimactic, like when a balloon deflates. She was even glad that she had screwed up so royally in the practice rounds, because it gave her the self-assurance that she could handle anything.

MEDALS ARE FOR CHILDREN

About the other goal! She did the math and in order to achieve the *80 x 80 Movement - Challenges for Life*, Haley would need to compete at a minimum in four events per year. Given that health and other circumstances might diminish her athletic capacity later in life, she felt that she should "front load" and complete events double-time the first few years.

What next? Will was going to be visiting with his girlfriend's family over Thanksgiving that year, so Haley signed the rest of the family up for the Mile High Turkey Trot. It was a blast picking out funny hats for them to wear to stand out in the crowd. Haley and Clint would wear turkey hats and she got a taco hat for Mattie. They would be two turkeys and a taco!

Clint had knee surgery that year, so he was going to be in the walking group. Mattie agreed to walk the course with her dad so that Haley could run ahead. When she finished, Haley lined up to receive her prize, only to be told that the medals were for children; the adults received a T-shirt.

She shared with the volunteer that she was competing in the **80 x 80 Movement - Challenges for Life** and that she needed the medal to prove that she had completed the race. The lady was adamant that if she gave her a medal, other adults would want one too—and what if they ran out of them? Then some children might not get one.

Haley finally relented and stepped away from the area to reflect on the true meaning of the accomplishment. It was to complete the event with her family, to make a contribution to the food bank by participating, and to live a full and healthy life. The medal really wasn't the purpose. It was a milestone crossed, and there was accomplishment and satisfaction in that as well, perhaps more so.

All of a sudden the volunteer tapped Haley on the shoulder and secretly gave her a medal. She shared how Haley's story really touched her. She said that Haley should be proud that she took on the **80 x 80 Movement - Challenges for Life** and that she wanted to recognize that accomplishment. So in the end Haley left feeling good about herself and went home with a medal.

POLISH HERE, SHINE THERE

The plan was to submit the professionally produced video of her eight-minute talk to other venues. Haley decided to apply to speaking engagements in locations where she wanted to visit friends or just have a chance to enjoy the area. It was already December, so this meant planning for the next year.

Haley received an unexpected email one week prior to the December Best Year Ever Blueprint (BYEB) held by Hal Elrod and Jon Berghoff in San Diego. It said that she was selected by the team to be one of five speakers at the event from the QLM group.

Remembering how she had been "voted off the stage" in the *America's Got Talent*-type competition in August, she was totally taken by surprise. And yet, this was the event Haley really wanted to present at. The TEDx stages offered the possibility for broad recognition. To Haley, though, her tribe was the people of BYEB and QLM.

Was she ever glad she had taken the time, resources, and energy to prepare her signature talk in advance! In later reflection, Moira pointed out that this was an example of "polish here, shine there." In other words, living true to one's vision by moving forward into one's future may unfold in ways one does not anticipate. In fact, it could be better. Haley thought, *What's good for me can actually be better for others, even the world.*

Chapter 11
FLIP TIME / LOVE LIFE

FLIP TIME / LOVE LIFE

Haley's message of "If you don't start now, then when?" resonated with the BYEB crowd. One lady even shouted, "Preach." At the idea of "flipping the pyramid" and starting with self-actualization, someone shouted, "YES." After Haley closed with the words, "If I can do it, you can too," Brotha James, Jon, and Hal jumped on stage to envelope her with huge hugs.

Those moments in time slowed down for Haley. It was like the words from *Slipstream: Time Hacking* by Benjamin Hardy: "The faster someone moves toward a desired destination, the slower time moves for them." Haley knew it was important to compress the highest quality and meaning of life into the time each person has to live.

Flip the Pyramid

Physiological Needs

Safety Needs

Belonging and Love Needs

Esteem Needs

Self
Actualization

LOOPING TIME

Haley reflected on her past: what if she could loop back and have a conversation with her younger self? What if that would make all the difference? Would she even listen to herself? What would she say that would make a difference? She remembered the words of Genevan philosopher, writer, and composer Jean-Jacques Rousseau: "The man who has lived the most is not he who has counted the most years, but he who has most felt life."

LEAPFROG

Next she leapfrogged to the future. Haley had a conversation with her future self. She projected who she wanted to BE, what she wanted to DO and HAVE in her life.

The words of Jim Rohn told her, "Don't wish it was easier. Wish you were better."

The realization that she couldn't change other people was a pivotal point. Along the same lines, she recognized that she couldn't change many circumstances. For example, although she was a successful mortgage lender for many years, she never was able to change interest rates or the market. Haley was surprised at how long it took her to realize that she only truly had control over herself.

Haley could control focusing on her self-actualization and living in her zone of genius. This truly was the most significant epiphany of all: the only person she could truly change was herself. And that meant the only one truly stopping her—was her.

What could she, would she, should she do differently now that would change the trajectory of her life, to create a new future?

MANIFESTO: 60 MISSION POSSIBLE

To celebrate her 60th year, Haley created a manifesto with the motto: 60 Mission Possible.

> BE: Highest and Best Self
> DO: Movement and Eat Well
> HAVE: Health
>
> BE: Highest and Best Self
> DO: Creative, Meaningful, and Valuable Work
> HAVE: Wealth and Prosperity
>
> BE: Highest and Best Self
> DO: Gratitude and Generosity
> HAVE: Happiness

#10YEARCHALLENGE

In 2019, social media platforms Facebook and Instagram exploded with #10YearChallenge. The idea was to post a photo from ten years ago and at present, a visual illustration of change. Haley recalled the words of American business magnate, investor, author, philanthropist, and humanitarian Bill Gates: "We always overestimate the change that will occur in the next two years and underestimate the change that will occur in the next ten. Don't let yourself be lulled into inaction."

Reflecting back on the decade, she remembered well the year she turned fifty. The year was 2009 and the market was extremely challenging, as the country was in the midst of the Great Recession. What stood out to Haley were not the deals lost and the challenging times. It was the people. The hiking vacation to Italy with Clint; visiting Will in Prague for his semester abroad; Mattie's horse Kiki being born on Haley's fiftieth birthday; and becoming partners with Anne. The time passed regardless. Why not create time for relationships, meaningful work, and activities?

LIFE LIST

Haley reflected that in *The Bucket List*, Carter shares that the Ancient Egyptians' God would ask two questions at the end of one's life:

- Have you found joy in your life?
- Has your life brought joy to others?

Haley created a list of what a life well-lived and full of meaning would consist of. She pictured her Heroine's Journey as a circle, and she confidently knew now that there was more transformation to come. Now, more than ever, she was a human BEING, rather than a human DOING. She was making a life while she made a living.

Her focus now was to BE love, DO generosity, and HAVE prosperity. She embodied the wisdom of the words of author, salesman, and motivational speaker Zig Ziglar: "You have to be before you can do, and do before you can have."

WHEN IF NOT NOW? WINN AT LIFE!

Haley came back to the now. Why did she feel like she had so much time, while others felt so busy? Didn't we all have the same twenty-four hours in each day?

On reflection, she realized that yes, we do all have twenty-four hours, but how the time is spent was quite different from person to person. She knew from her experiences that the Heroine's Journey was an inside job and it was continuous and cyclical—that's why it was configured as a circle rather than a straight line. Where are you on the Heroine's Journey? Your gifts, like Haley's, are unique, one of a kind.

In the book, *The Top Five Regrets of the Dying*, Bronnie Ware, an Australian palliative care nurse, shares that the top epiphany expressed by those in her care: "I wish I'd had the courage to live a life true to myself, not the life others expected of me." NOW is the time; there may not be a later.

WHAT ONE FOCUSES ON EXPANDS

Now you, too, know the secrets of how to love the life you have while you create and co-create the life of your dreams. Remember, what one focus on expands. You will start experiencing the benefits of it, just like Haley did, and want to do more. Time expands as you live into your zone of genius.

Dreams do come true, and they can happen to you. Haley started when she was fifty. And if she can do it, so can you! Your challenge is, starting today, right now, to commit to investing in your personal development. Do something meaningful that you have been wanting to do. Do you know what it will be?

If you don't start now, when? You can start at any time! If Haley can do it, so can you! Start today!

For more inspiration on your Flip Time / Love Life journey, watch Karen Briscoe's talk to BYEB at: www.5minutesuccess.com

Chapter 12
REFLECTIONS ON THE HEROINE'S JOURNEY

One of Haley's all-time favorite movies is *The **Wizard** of Oz*. As a young girl, she was frightened by the Wicked Witch of the West and her flying monkeys. Now that she knows more about the Heroine's Journey and recognizes that she has been living it herself, she took time to reflect on the characters in her life and how they relate to the Land of Oz. Clearly she, like Dorothy, is the protagonist.

How fortuitous that even the meaning of Haley's name is heroine. Although the heroine makes do with her life, she feels as if something is missing, a sense of discomfort or tension. Dorothy knows she needs to make a change. She wishes upon a star, sings about "somewhere over the rainbow" and ponders "why, oh why, can't I?"

A twister throws Dorothy into the Land of Oz. For the rest of the journey, she seeks to find her way back home to Kansas. The process is a metamorphosis, like the simple caterpillar becoming a gorgeous butterfly.

The enemy or nemesis for Dorothy is none other than the Wicked Witch of the West. For Haley, it is time; it seems that there is never enough. She feels as though she is in a constant state of overwhelm and "too busy" to accomplish anything meaningful.

In the movie, the Good Witch, Glinda, represents the "still small voice." In Haley's life, the person who acts as a guide to "follow her own yellow brick road" is Moira. As a life and executive coach, she shows Haley that she has the power within her all along. This guidance is more intuitive, which is creative and spiritual. Outer guides are those people in our lives who connect thoughts back to love and one's true self. The words attributed to Buddha Siddhartha Guatama Shakyamuni and the Theosophists ring true: "When the student is ready, the teacher will appear." Just like Dorothy, all Haley needed to do was to click her red heels, twirl around a few times, and state, "There's no place like home."

True "home" for Haley exists when she lives in her zone of genius. When by her thoughts, actions, and vision she embodies the affirmation to love the life she has while she creates and co-creates the life of her dreams. The people along the journey for Dorothy and Haley represent the folks who bear gifts that also serve as life lessons. Friends use their knowledge, skills, and abilities to rescue Dorothy and to help her escape the clutches of the Wicked Witch and her guards. Haley encounters helpful friends, as well, on her journey to discover her true self.

The Cowardly Lion's gift is courage. Haley found the two most impactful encouragers of her life to be her two business partners, Audrey and Anne. In terms of demographics, one was about fifteen years older and the other the same on the younger end of the spectrum. In a way, those two ladies serve as bookends to Haley's journey as both friends and advocates.

The Scarecrow's gift is brains. The intellectual challenge of inspirational mentors Hal Elrod, Jon Berghoff, and Gay Hendricks elevated Haley's business and life to new levels. A lifelong learner and reader, Haley possesses an insatiable desire to grow.

The Tin Man's gift is a heart. For Haley, without a doubt, that includes her immediate family of Clint, Will, and Mattie. It also encompasses her "work" family of team members, staff, clients, and community. They were her "big why" and gave reason to achieve the team mission to impact and improve people's lives.

The protagonist meets with challenges along her journey. The Wizard, the Great and Powerful Oz, agrees to grant their wishes as long as they pass the tests he issues. Dorothy is to bring back the Wicked Witch's broomstick. The others, along with Dorothy, are to face their greatest enemy—their fear.

In the classic story, the Wicked Witch of the West writes in the sky: *Surrender Dorothy*. The profound words serve a dual message. The Witch's intent is to illicit fear and serve as a warning. And yet the flip side is that once one surrenders to her true self, no green-faced Witch, winged monkey army, or fake Wizard can ever take away one's worthiness.

For Haley, it is her Inner Critic that she faces to achieve her vision to live into her full potential. The Inner Critic has been her own personal prosecuting attorney, critical, fear-based, and judgmental. Her accomplishments, attitude, and actions seem to be always on trial. Both Dorothy and Haley learn that they have it within them all along. By tapping into their curiosity and inner resources, they are able to achieve their heart's desire.

The trickster for Dorothy is Toto, her little dog. Recall in the story how Toto would do things that put Dorothy in jeopardy. The Wicked Witch takes Toto and Dorothy goes to rescue her pet. In one pivotal scene, Toto escapes and Dorothy is left behind. The Wicked Witch turns over an hourglass to show how much time Dorothy has left. Her friends come to rescue her as the final grains of sand in the hourglass trickle down.

Haley feels the time in the hourglass as her trickster. In many ways, she is blessed and has lived a full life. And yet, at over the half-century mark, she recognizes that there is likely less time on the other side.

Dorothy and the others do as the Wizard asks and return with evidence. He bellows to come back tomorrow and Dorothy says, "If you are really great and powerful, you would keep your promises." Toto scoots away and pulls the curtain back to reveal that Oz is just a man who operates a dashboard of cinematic effects. It is merely the appearance of power. Dorothy calls him out on his ruse, and he responds that he is a good man, just a very bad wizard.

The protagonist is change and there is no going back. Glinda helps

Dorothy recognize the epiphany that she doen't need to be helped any longer. She always possessed the power to return to Kansas. Glinda didn't tell her earlier because she wouldn't have believed her. Dorothy had to discover it for herself that "home" is what she makes of it in her mind.

Haley, too, discovers she has possessed the power within her the entire time. She just had to click her red sparkly shoes three times, twirl around, and say there's no place like home. Each time she goes through the Heroine's Journey, it becomes faster, easier, and more fun! Just as Moira assured her it would.

Dorothy realizes that it isn't enough to want to see her family; if she ever seeks her heart's desire again, she will start first in her own backyard. If it isn't there, then she never really lost it to begin with.

There is truly no place like home—which is to BE your highest and best self. Home is a place one belongs, where we can be the person we are called to be.

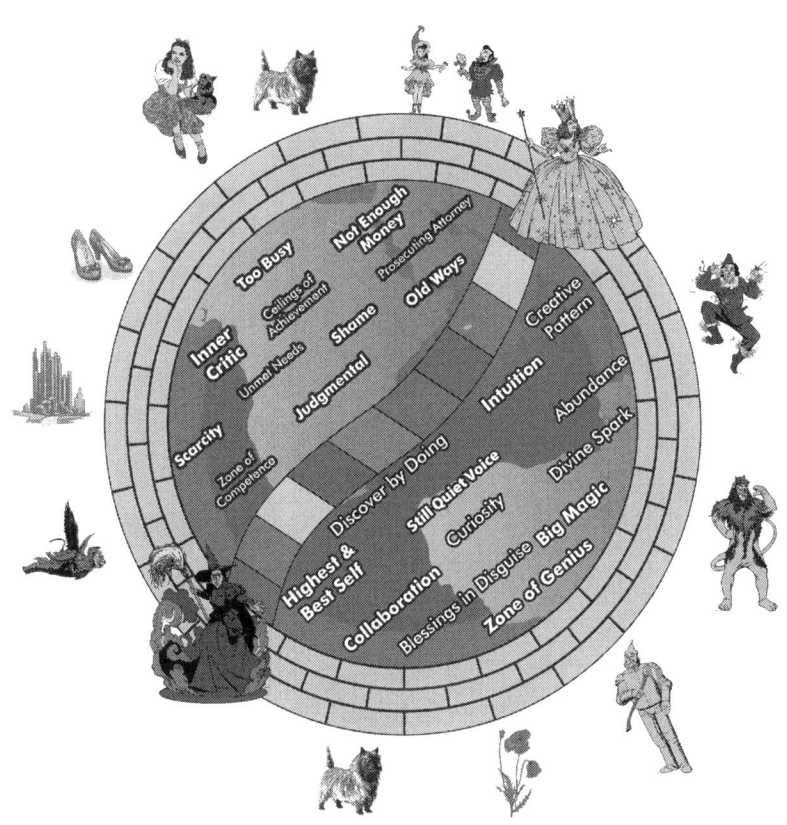

CHARACTER LIST

Haley Beck	The protagonist
Clint Beck	Haley's husband
Will and Mattie	Haley and Clint's kids
Audrey Adler	Seasoned business partner who Haley purchased company from
Anne Crawford	Younger business partner who joined Haley
Jenny	Friend from coaching group who wants to open a cooking school
Lizzy	Friend from coaching group who wants to offer yoga for preschool students
Christina	Friend from coaching group who wants to produce documentary movies
Lewis and Rosemary Fuller	Haley's parents
Heath and Emily	Will's friends getting married

Invite Karen to Speak

www.5minutesuccess.com

About the Author

Karen Briscoe is the creator of the *5 Minute Success* concept. She regularly speaks on a national and local level on the best of *5 Minute Success* and *Flip Time / Love Life*. Further, she is the host of the *5 Minute Success* podcast, which has an amazing array of guests, which achieve success at a high level in business and life. She has completed the John Maxwell Team Certification Program for Coaching, Speaking, and Training.

Karen is a frequent guest on other podcasts and webinars that focus on entrepreneurial success and motivation, as well as real estate-related topics. She is also a contributing author to real estate media outlets *INMAN* and *Real Trends*.

Karen Briscoe is principal owner of the Huckaby Briscoe Conroy Group (HBC) with Keller Williams, located in McLean, Virginia. The HBC Group has been recognized by *The Wall Street Journal* as one of the 250 Top Realtor® teams in the United States. Since 1977, HBC Group has sold more than 1,500 homes valued at more than $1.5 billion. The team consistently sells over one hundred residential properties annually, ranging from multi-million-dollar luxury estates to condominiums and townhomes. Primary market areas include Northern Virginia, suburban Maryland, and Washington, DC.

Karen began her real estate career developing residential lots with the Trammell Crow Company in Dallas, Texas. In Northern Virginia, she worked in commercial real estate with The Staubach Company prior to entering residential sales. Karen earned a master's degree from Southern Methodist University in Dallas, Texas and received her BA from Stephens College in Columbia, Missouri—her hometown.

She attributes her life worth living to God, her husband Andy, children Drew and Callie, her family, and countless friends and business associates. Her family is actively involved at Trinity United Methodist Church in McLean, Virginia.

Karen is available to speak to your organization, group, company, or association.

5 Minute Success -
The Podcast

Want to flip time so that you love the life you have while you create and co-create the life of your dreams? Do you want to achieve success at a higher level in business and life by investing just 5 minutes a day?

Connect with Karen and the **5 Minute Success** and **Flip Time** community!

- **Subscribe** to **5 Minute Success - The Podcast** on iTunes, Google Play, Stitcher, Overcast and other players.

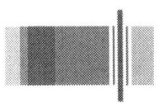  

Also by **Karen Briscoe**

Real Estate Success in 5 Minutes a Day:
Secrets of a Top Agent Revealed

Coming Soon:
Success in 5 Minutes a Day 66 Day Challenge®

Consult to Sell: 66 Day Challenge®

66 days to Focus on this Core Topic from the Original
Real Estate Success in 5 Minutes a Day

Connect to Build and Grow: 66 Day Challenge®

66 days to Focus on this Core Topic from the Original
Real Estate Success in 5 Minutes a Day

Success Thinking, Activities & Vision: 66 Day Challenge®

66 days to Focus on this Core Topic from the Original
Real Estate Success in 5 Minutes a Day

Success in 5 Minutes a Day
by Concept Authors:

Savvy Woman Success in 5 Minutes a Day
By Moira Lethbridge

For a complete listing of other products visit
www.5MinuteSuccess.com
Also by **Karen Briscoe**

Get Social with
5 Minute Success & FLIP TIME!

5 Minute Success:
Website: www.5MinuteSuccess.com
Facebook Group: https://www.facebook.com/groups/5minutesuccess/

Flip Time:
Website: http://fliptimelovelife.com/
Facebook: https://www.facebook.com/groups/fliptimelovelife/

80x80 Movement - Milestones & Medals - Challenges for Life:
Website: http://www.80x80Movement.com/
Facebook: https://www.facebook.com/groups/80x80Movement

Made in the USA
Columbia, SC
29 August 2019